Ways to Learn

David Bouchard

Literacy Consultants
David Booth • Kathleen Corrigan

It is good to learn.

Learning is fun.

There are many ways to learn.

Friends can play.

Friends can teach.

People learn from their friends.

Families can laugh.

Families can teach.

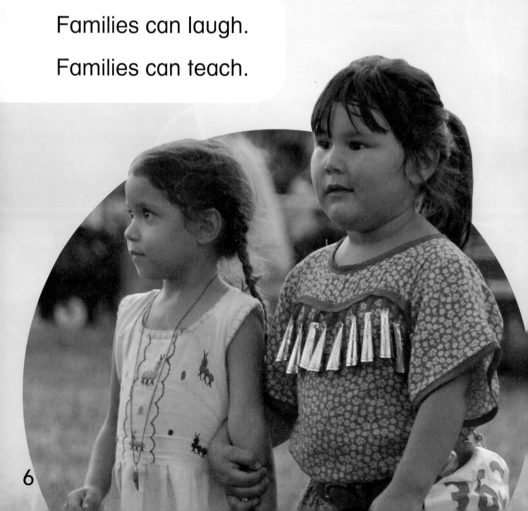

People learn from their family.

The community can share.

The community can teach.

People learn from the community.

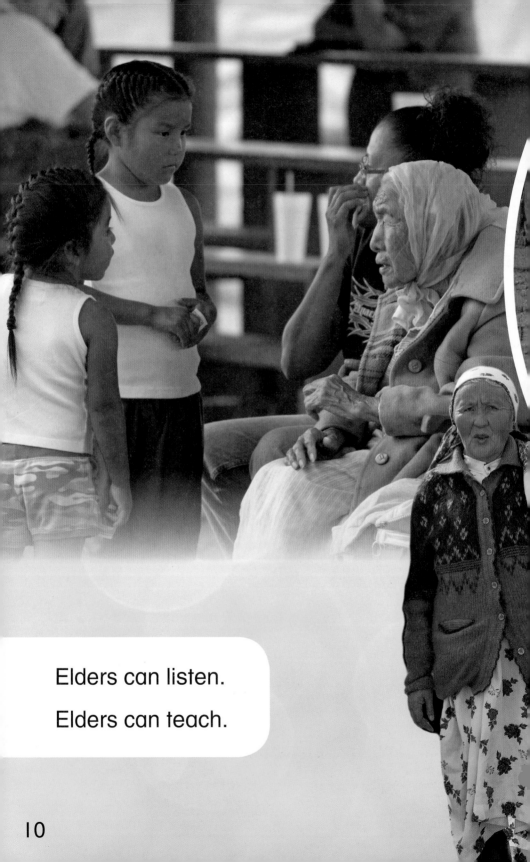

Elders can listen.

Elders can teach.

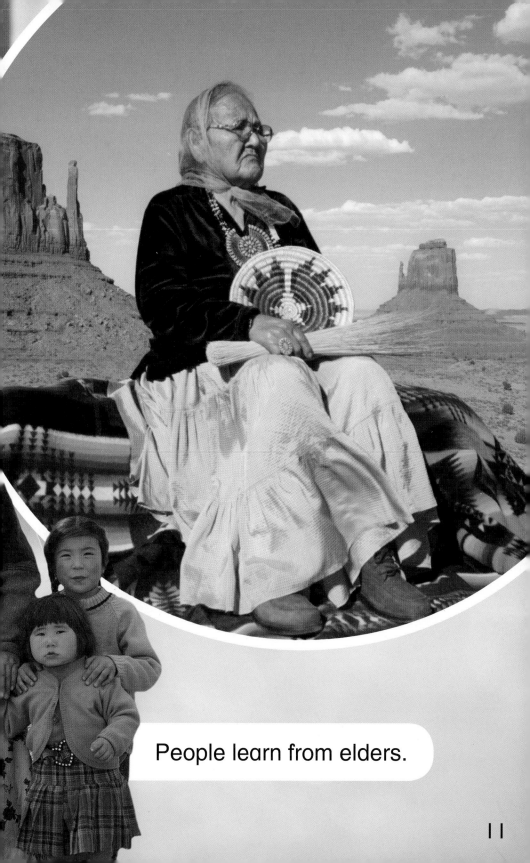

People learn from elders.

People can learn from nature.

People learn from the sun.

People learn from the moon.

People learn from the animals.

Friends can teach.

Family can teach.

The community can teach.

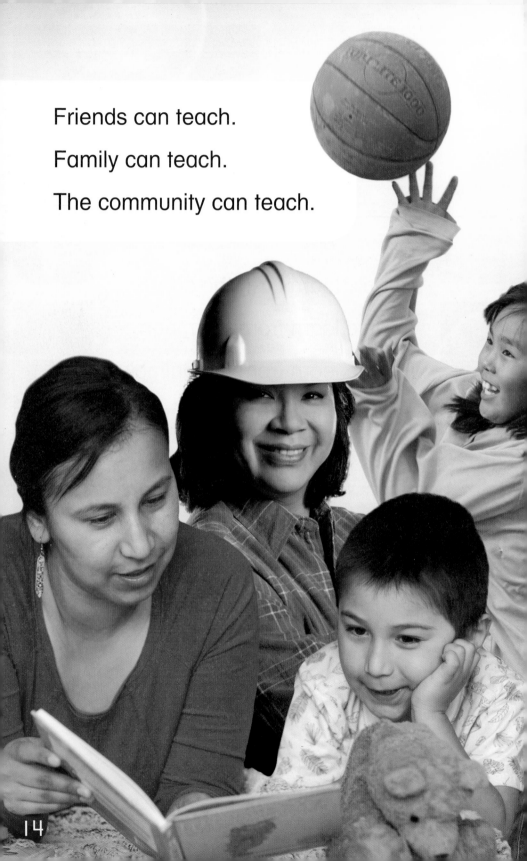

Nature can teach.

Animals can teach.

Elders can teach too.

There are many ways to learn.